God's Spies

Joanna Infeld

Printed in the United States of America

Kora Press ® is a federally registered trademark.
ISBN (10) 0-9815509-6-7
ISBN (13) 978-0-9815509-6-1

Cover photo by Joanna Infeld

Published by Kora Press ®
KoraPress.com

New York, New York

God's Spies

Gratefully Aging

Joanna Infeld

By the same author:

7 Ages of Woman
In-Tuition; Moments of Awakening
In-Formation; Moments of Realization
In-Sight; Moments of Being
Empowering Women
Dear Gabriel; Letters From a Trainee Angel
Unmasked; Spirit Flares

All are available from www.KoraPress.com and www.EnergyWorlds.com.

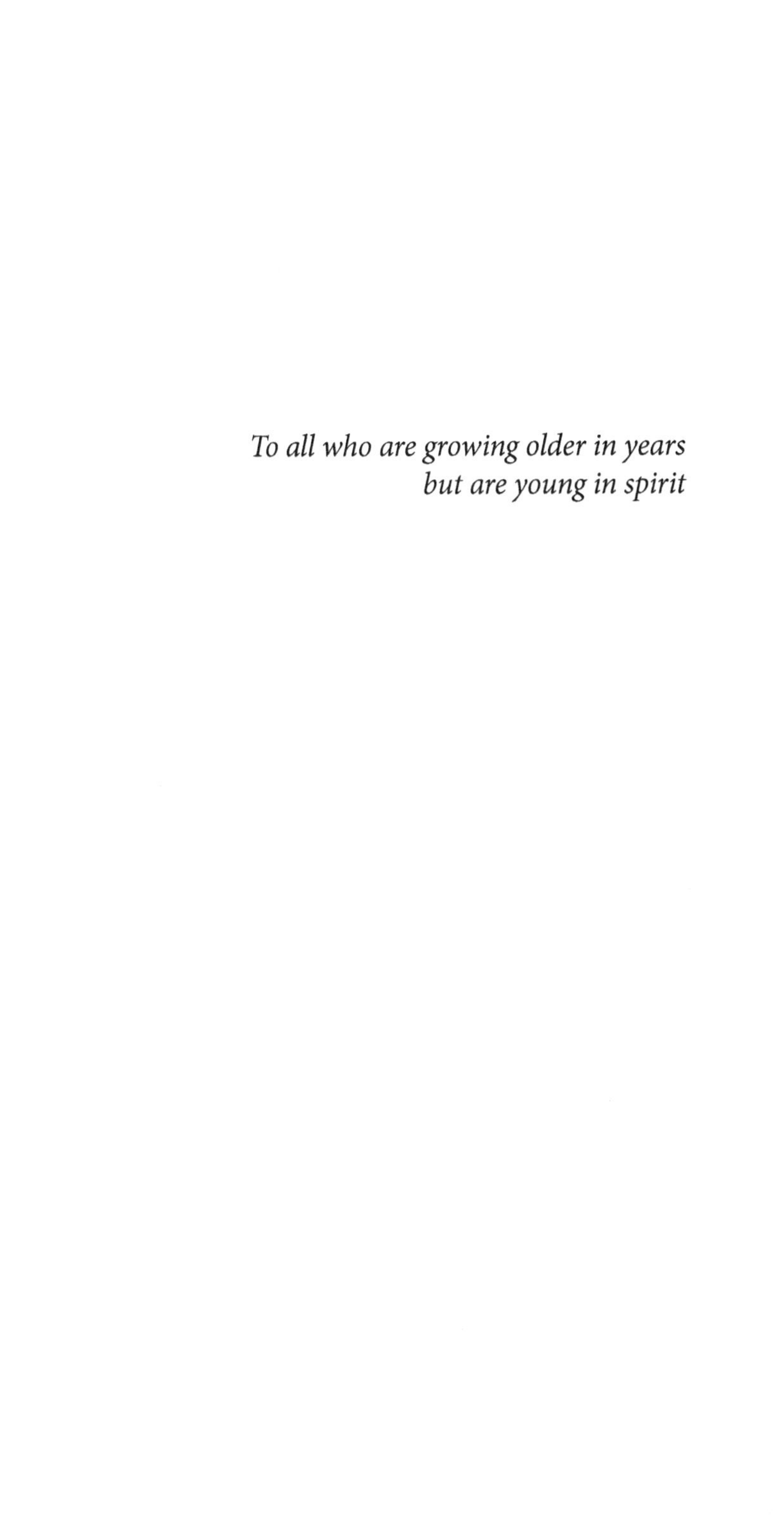

To all who are growing older in years
but are young in spirit

We look at life with fading eyes;
We see the folly and the try.
When to laugh and when to cry?
We reserve our judgement,
Because we are God's spies.

We two alone will sing like birds i' the cage:
When thou dost ask me blessing, I'll kneel down
And ask of thee forgiveness: so we'll live,
And pray, and sing, and tell old tales, and laugh
At gilded butterflies, and hear poor rogues
Talk of court news; and we'll talk with them too,
Who loses and who wins; who's in, who's out;
And talk upon's the mystery of things,
As if we were God's spies.

William Shakespeare
King Lear, Act V, Scene 1

Contents

Introduction

At the time of writing this book I am in my 70th year. So my body is 69 years old, but I believe the spirit is immortal and ageless. As I approach the exit, I wonder about my future. I also marvel at the gift of old age. When younger I used to think that once one achieved old age, life somehow would come to a halt. I remember sitting in school and wondering what I would be like at fifty-six, being that I had calculated I would become that age by the turn of the century. I imagined I would slow down, lose interest in my surroundings and retreat into my memories of the past. That is how I saw old age to be. Yet I have been surprised that the opposite is true. I feel an urgency to accomplish what I have been sent here onto this planet to achieve. I know that my remaining time is short and there is so much more for me to do. So rather than slowing down, I feel I am speeding up.

There is so much that I have seen and done; I, as all old people, have been witness to a time and to events that will never be repeated in the same way again. It is my sacred duty to share my wisdom and document my memories for future generations.

I marvel at the love I have experienced and witnessed. I believe love is the highest form of energetic exchange between humans and the sacred substance that one is able to take with one when the time to exit this planet comes. I believe that we are meant to collect and process fine qualities, such as love, compassion, patience and care, which will become our passport into our future.

This is my swan song. Although I intend to write many more books and articles before I die, this one is about me now and old age, and the many aspects of entering and growing through the crowning years.

This is how I wrote about the final stage of life in the book *Seven Ages of Woman*, where I likened each stage of life to a color of the rainbow, and where old age is described as being violet:

VIOLET (67-77 and beyond)

Finally violet surprises you
with its urgency at core
and keeps you trying to improve
and asking for more.
So then as the end approaches,
you know what life is about:
to discover your purpose and eradicate doubt,
to learn and assist others, help lighten their load,
to grow quality and qualities on this earthly road.

I believe there is a new breed of humans on planet Earth. They are older and wiser, and at the same time they are physically agile and mentally aware. Some people say sixty is the new fifty and seventy is the new sixty. Whatever the description, we defy the old people's home and are taking on the role of teachers and mentors. We will pass on fully aware of what is happening to us, having prepared for departure. We see life to be a journey into our next incarnation, whatever that will turn out to be.

Contemplation 1

Consider a place that you liked, where you felt at home. It can be a friend's house, a restaurant, an ancient monument or place in nature; it can be a beach, a mountain, a lake or forest. It can be a busy street, a shop or museum.

Think for a moment why you felt comfortable there. Find a word, a few words or a phrase to describe it. Perhaps you will learn something about yourself and perhaps the words used to describe your special place will also define an aspect of your character and energy field that you might not have even been aware of before now.

What attracts you to a place is an aspect of your own energy field that is similar in nature and compatible with it. Part of you belongs to this place because you would happily *be* here for a *long* time. The energy of this place is food for you, because your energy is compatible with it so that there is an energy exchange between you and it.

When you feel energetically depleted, think about your special place and perhaps you will feel it energize you, as its frequency flows into you along the wire established and grown through this contemplation.

Gratefully Aging

When I was finishing this book, I spent some time, with the help of my husband David, looking for a short and pithy subtitle that would explain in a few words what the book is about. We felt it was necessary, being that not everyone will have the reference to Shakespeare's quote from *King Lear* about God's spies.

I initially I thought of the words "Aging With Grace," but it seemed that this book could then be misconstrued to be a Christian religious handbook. It is important to me that these writings are non-denominational, as I want them to appeal to anyone who is approaching the crowning years, no matter what their religious persuasion or beliefs might be. So I changed the words around and added "Gracefully Aging" to the cover. After I had done that, the cover file was open on my computer screen, as I was testing the new sub-title and wondering about its appeal to the potential reader of the book.

As David was walking by, he looked at the screen and said, "I saw the words *Gratefully Aging*." So we changed one letter—a *c* to a *t* and we both felt that this was it—just one letter had been changed and everything fell into place.

Sometimes that is all it takes—one small adjustment, and an attitude, a mood or a thought pattern can be changed and elevated in a moment. That is what this book is about—short writings to help a person come to terms with the fact of aging and to draw from their experience the lessons and the richness that is available to them. I believe old age is a gift to be enjoyed and lived to the fullest extent possible.

Being grateful is a key to health, joy and happiness. A moment of being grateful in the morning can flavor your whole day. Just like a homeopathic remedy, a drop of grateful essence will brighten your world and keep you energetically buoyant 24/7.

Here is a list of things to be grateful for:

I AM GRATEFUL FOR:

1. Being alive
2. Having food to eat
3. Having shelter
4. Companionship
5. Health
6. Work
7. Creativity

The Impermanence of All Things

One of the greatest benefits of getting older is being able to appreciate the impermanence of all things. As time passes, it becomes known that all will pass and that eventually every house, every building, every tree and every single person we know and see around us will eventually be gone.

When an older person says to a youngster, "Life is short," there is no way an adolescent or young adult can appreciate this statement, because for them becoming grown up is a long journey that lasts a lifetime. But for an older person it is self evident that the years had gone by almost imperceptibly and that there is precious little time left. Now is the time to make that remaining time meaningful and to think about and contribute to one's legacy.

What does an older person want? Health is high on the list because without health little can be done or appreciated. Then there is finding those special activities that bring joy and satisfaction to one's dwindling days. And finally there is the ability to share precious moments and memories with one's family and loved ones. Everything else, like material possessions or the acquisition of wealth fade into the background of one's life as they lose their luster and become seen and understood as the impermanent support to our lives that they really are.

Of course, if there is no financial security and a person does not have a retirement fund or other means of survival, then fending for oneself becomes a major concern as the ability to work and earn a living lessens for most people as they grow older. But, if maintenance has been secured, the importance of material possessions will fade in comparison with the richness of experience and memories. Material possessions become less important because an older person knows they will not be taking them with them when the time comes. They are also not concerned so much with outward appearance, because mostly they no longer wish to impress others or are looking for a date or romance. Yes, of course they want to still look young and neat and tidy, and especially women might still be coloring their hair and putting make-up on daily. But it is unlikely they will be buying the latest fashion in clothes or new trendy boots. Shoes especially will be chosen for their comfort.

Old age is a good time to get rid of clutter. As a person ages and no longer needs to wear the power suit or presentable clothes one used to put on to go to work, the closets become filled with more comfortable attire. If some item has not been worn for a year or more (which means that a person has managed without it through all four seasons), it probably means that it will never be worn again and it is time to take it to the thrift store or give it away to someone who might enjoy it. Books that have not been read and have been on the shelf for years can be donated to a local library where they can still be accessible if ever the time comes to read them.

All other possessions are ours only as long as we are here in the physical body and able to use them. Once we are gone, our carefully collected jewelry, furniture, clothes, books and all other possessions will be dispersed and distributed within a matter of days.

These days I look at my surroundings and I see that all of it is on loan. I feel grateful for the facility they have afforded me, whether they have accompanied me for a lifetime or whether they have been with me for mere days or weeks.

As a person grows older, they see more and more changes. Governments rise and fall, country borders change and everything that might have seemed stable and unmovable at the time changes, alters, transforms or disappears altogether.

From the age of seven I grew up and was educated in communist Poland. At the time it did not seem that the mode of government would ever change, despite the fact that just like in any totalitarian regime, it satisfied only a privileged few. And yet, if you visit Poland today, it is quite a different country and the Warsaw of my youth no longer exists, except within my memories and the memories of those who lived there at the time and are still alive today.

All civilizations develop and decline, according, as some researches have suggested, to the cycles of the sun. We, too, are subject to cycles as we pass through the ages from birth to departure: childhood, adolescence, youth, mid-life and the senior years.

Living With Change and Changing to Live

Getting older and growing up affects all parts of a person—their body, their soul, their mind and their spirit. Although many changes are visible, it is the changes in the energy field that are the most dramatic. One can see on *YouTube* a number of examples of daily photographs taken over a period of 10 years allowing the viewer to observe a child's growth over a decade within the timespan of a few minutes.

Anyone who has lived for half a century or longer has observed major changes happening all around them. Perhaps change is imperceptible from day-to-day, but looking over a decade or two, change becomes more obvious. The development of technology, communications and the Internet are major advancements that we have witnessed in our times. And yet there are also subtle changes that have revolutionized our life. For example, I still marvel at the fact that when I was younger and started to travel, no one had invented suitcases with wheels. We all carried our own luggage or hired a porter to help us with the heavy burden. Shoes were fastened mostly with laces or zippers, because we were not privy to the use of Velcro—an invention brought to 20th-century civilization by the Swiss electrical engineer George de Mestral, basing his discovery on his observation of how burrs could stick to clothing without glue. Bottled water is another necessity of life that has now become accepted and required by modern culture, to avoid water pollution and to remain safe and healthy, rather than risking to imbibe H_2O from the tap, which these days contains chlorine, fluoride and/or other unhealthy pollutants.

But above all, the number of people currently alive on planet Earth has increased exponentially—it has doubled to seven billion from three and a half in 1968. In my lifetime the number of humans has more than doubled; it has tripled. And although the effect of this growth can be best seen and felt in such countries as India or Bangladesh, there are more people everywhere.

The symbolically chosen six billionth person on Earth was born on October 31st, 1999. Identified by the UN, his name is Adnan Mevic and he was born in Sarajevo in Bosnia. When he was two days old he was visited in hospital by Kofi Annan, Secretary General of the United Nations and his photograph was published around the globe. On his twelfth birthday there were another billion people added to the world's population. The UN named the seven billionth child to be Danica May Camacho, born on October 31st, 2012 in the Philippines.

It is most probable that I will live to see the eight billionth person to be born, or even the ninth. But growth has reached its peak and is now slowing down. Scientists predict future numbers based on past cycles of growth, but no one really knows the future. This is what makes living so exciting—the unpredictability of it all. If there is one thing I have learned in this lifetime, it is that change is occurring all the time and the outcome of any forecasts is dubious at best because reality will always surpass predictions and human expectations.

The United Nations commented on the birth of the seven billionth child that it *"is a challenge, an opportunity and a call to action. Our record population size can be viewed in many ways as a success for humanity because it means that people are living longer and more of our children are surviving worldwide. But not everyone has benefited from this achievement or the higher quality of life that this implies."*

Current world population growth is 78 million a year, which is about the current size of Germany. This is one aspect of change that affects all people on Earth and will continue to have an impact on economic growth, natural resources, energy consumption, global warming and all aspects of our lives throughout our century.

More people also means more brain power, more competition, more human energy exchange and manufacture. We are not alone and among seven billion people we never will be.

Approaching the Exit

I want to cross over, I want to go home
But she says, Go back, go back to the world.

Leonard Cohen,
The Night Comes On

One way of looking at the fact of growing older is that one is approaching the exit. Like sitting in a waiting room, waiting for the results of a medical test, one becomes aware that the end is nigh. Depending on one's belief system, this can be a fear or a cause for hope and anticipation or even relief. The question inevitably arises, will the next life be better than this one? Will I come back to this planet or reincarnate elsewhere? What if I reincarnated back in time? Is that even possible? If I reincarnate forward onto the Earth, what will life be like by the time I am grown up, say in the 2040s, or 50s or 60s?

Will I know the people I am currently friends with? Will I be related to the same family? Will learning be easier the next time around? And what about people who do not believe in reincarnation? Do they get the same opportunities? Do Christians go to a different place than Muslims or Jews? Do Buddhists achieve nirvana? If there is a heaven, what is it like? What could the worst hell be like? Are heaven and hell real?

Researches believe that in ancient Egypt people were very aware of the journey awaiting them after their earthly life was over. They knew where they were going to reincarnate and had the color spectrum associated with their chosen star destination painted on the side of their sarcophagi. Much of their waking hours was taken up with preoccupation with life after death and spiritual ceremonies.

As one grows older, one's beliefs become challenged because there is no guarantee—no one has come back to say what the other side was like. Yes, there are those who have had near-death or out-of-body experiences, but those memories only go so far because no one has been dead for more than a few minutes and come back to describe the afterlife. If we are to believe the reports of those who had suffered clinical death and consequently been revived, there are several stages to the near-death experience. First there is a tunnel that leads to a bright light. It is like moving towards a different dimension or an alternative reality. Then there is entering the white light. Different people interpret it in different ways. Christians see Jesus Christ, Buddhists see Buddha and Muslims see Mohammed. But all report the feeling of compassion and peace. Mostly when people are told that they need to go back, they do so reluctantly and usually it is only because they have unfinished business here on Earth. Perhaps there is a child that needs looking after or an injured spouse. Those who return usually say they would rather have stayed within the feeling of bliss and contentment they had experienced while they were clinically dead. It is only a sense of duty that brings them back. It is also curious that after their near-death experience, mostly people are no longer afraid of death but see it as a welcome change of state they often look forward to, as a release from struggle and pain.

The next stage is being greeted and welcomed by deceased family members and loved ones. Sometimes these people—parents, lovers, friends who had passed before—are waiting in the tunnel; sometimes they are there as one emerges into the bright light.

Then there is the life review. This is when a person gains better understanding of the consequences of one's deeds and thoughts. Moments which seemed insignificant while alive here on Earth might acquire unexpected significance, like, for example, the fact of rescuing a bird with a broken wing or taking the initiative and apologizing to someone for some little hurt one had inflicted on another person either through carelessness or stupidity. Even moments long forgotten can now become refreshed and presented in a new light. People report that the life review feels like an unbiased assessment of one's actions and words on planet Earth—there is no guilt or regret, just an understanding that if one were to be given one's time again one would do things differently. One is not judged by some higher authority; one simply acquires a better understanding of one's actions and deeds.

This life review is one aspect of life after death that perhaps starts even before one dies. As one gets older, one tends to look back on one's life, searching for trends, cycles and moments when one's character manifested most clearly and when development had occurred. Every person has these defining moments; remembering them they are able to gain insight into the motivation that has moved and still moves their life and propels them into action or radical change.

For example, most people have those moments when they unexpectedly meet someone who then plays a significant part in their life or when they discover a group or organization that influences their beliefs. They might wonder what was it that had propelled them to the exact place and time to be able to meet that person or group. There is no easy answer to this, but if everything consists of and emanates energy, then according to the law of energy attraction, like attracts like. This concept has become known as the Law of Attraction.

Serendipity is more than a chance meeting or coincidence. Throughout our life, as we are drawn to certain people, places and events, other people and circumstances become attracted to us. Perhaps coincidences are not by chance, they are co-incidences of two energies coming together that might have been traveling towards each other for days, years or even decades.

How does it happen that of all the people on earth, we meet the person we eventually marry? What causes us to live in the precise house or apartment we make our home? What makes us choose a specific college, town or place of work where we might consequently spend years of our life? And conversely, why do we decline other job offers, marriage proposals or invitations?

As we get to know ourselves better over the years, we become more attuned to people and places that are compatible with our own energy field. An older person will most probably not waste time in an abusive relationship or go to places that make them feel uncomfortable. After years of trial and error, a senior will know what is food for them and what is dangerous poison to their systems, both physically and energetically.

Energetic Senses

One of the aspects of growing older is that the physical senses tend to dull (become less sharp). Mostly it is noticeable when the eyesight and hearing become less acute, but taste, smell and even touch can be affected as well. However, the five equivalent energetic senses become better developed with age, which means that the older a person gets, the more attuned they become to the subtle realms. Their instincts are on the alert and in self preservation mode, which is why older people often can predict the future or the outcome of an event. This is not to say that they suddenly become psychic, but due to experience and the years of meeting and getting to know people, they tend to have an almost uncanny ability to sense the nature of another person or to assess a situation they find themselves in.

So they might be the ones who warn a younger person of the dangers of getting involved with someone whose intentions might be less than honorable; they might anticipate the worst when traveling to a foreign land. They might also be more cautious when venturing into a new business deal or sale transaction.

An older person has been *in tuition* for their entire life. Now is the time to listen to one's *intuition* and become sensitive to the promptings from within. This sixth sense is also a prompting as to what can go right. An older person has experienced both extremes—the good and the bad. Caution is one outcome resulting from over half a century of experience, but optimism and hope is another. Both possibilities live side by side; it is up to the person and their attitude to make the difference.

"There are many dangers in this world, and the longer one journeyed through life the more one understood how varied these dangers were. That, thought Mma Ramotswe, was why one worried more and more about others: one could imagine the manifold disasters that might befall them."

"We get more frightened as we get older, Mma... More and more frightened—of everything."

Mma Ramotswe nodded. But why? Because we had so many things go wrong in our lifetime?

The Miracle at Speedy Motors
Alexander McCall Smith
Anchor Books, 2008, New York, New York

Religion

The older I get, the further I move away from established religion. More and more I see the contradictions between the theory and the practice, between what is preached and the behavior of those who preach. I love Bill Maher's idea of *"the religion of doubt."* I believe we should implement our reasoning faculty to discover for ourselves what we believe in and what is hogwash, invented by the purveyors of religion who are trying to keep control over their "flocks."

My father was born a Jew but lost his faith in his teenage years and became a scientist (he was a one of Einstein's collaborators—they wrote the book *The Evolution of Physics* together). My mother was an atheist; her mother was an Irish Roman Catholic who had lost her faith and her father was a German Protestant. From the age of seven I grew up in a Poland, which is a Catholic country and where I joined my friends and went to church on Sunday, praying to a Christian God, to Jesus and the Catholic saints.

I do believe that there is intelligent life in the Universe and that life has meaning and purpose, but I do not believe I need a priest or a rabbi to be an intermediary between me and a higher power. I do have a lot of respect those who study scripture and attempt to penetrate the mysteries of the Universe with their minds or through meditation.

Existing religions started with a single person who became a prophet. But all prophets are now gone and if they lived today, they would probably alter their teachings to adjust to these times. Jesus Christ was a Jew, but he introduced new ideas and new teachings which he shared with his disciples. *The New Testament* contains stories about his ministry. *The New Testament* is no longer new; it is over 2,000 years old. What would a new new testament be like?

All religions have gems of wisdom, and I would not want to reject any of them in favor of one. The world's religious heritage is rich in wisdom and writings that give food for thought and contain useful advice on how to live a life. There is much to explore and learn and to make up one's mind about.

I believe that in the end, every person achieves their own version of universal truth. It is our privilege to construct our own moral and spiritual code of conduct, behavior and belief. I believe an open mind is the best companion an older person can hope for. It leaves the door open for new discoveries and revelations which will occur if you let them.

Belief is a thread that connects us to the unseen worlds of energy and to the future. Throughout our life we construct a belief system, based on our education and experience; it can give us hope and sustain us in times of turmoil and trouble. I believe that the Universe has been constructed with love and compassion and that the phrase *"the human is made in the image of God"* means that we are capable of love, compassion and creativity which are godly and sacred qualities.

Collecting Qualities

As a person's final days approach, they will want to gather to themselves as many fine qualities as possible, perhaps instinctively knowing that these are the only possessions they can take with them when they depart from this life and enter the next. You might ask, how do you collect such qualities as honor, peace, hope or humility? There is only one way: by giving them away.

For example, an older person finds it easier to state their feelings for their spouse, siblings or their children. They are no longer afraid of rejection and they want to give their love away, before it is too late, so they can have more of it when they have to leave their loved ones behind. Often an older person will seek forgiveness from a person they might have hurt in the past. Knowing that they now have absolution, whether they are religious or not, will make their departure an easier passage.

During the crowning years a person has the opportunity to gather to themselves the best of who they had been throughout their life. Each memory contains within it the gems that make up a person's character. Often older people will recount their stories time and time again, because each time they repeat an anecdote or description of an incidence, they recapture the essence of that moment, and are able to once again live through it and reconnect to the energies contained therein. This is food for the soul, and at an older age the soul is nourished more from inside than from outside.

Youth gathers experiences and impressions from the outside in, whereas older people have developed their own internal landscape which nourishes and sustains them. An older person's hall of memories is vast; within it are stories, lessons, anecdotes and endearments. For almost every story heard, an older person will have another story on the same subject to tell. Seniors are the story tellers of our culture, for they are the custodians of the history of the human tribe.

GOING HOME

Going home
Without my sorrow
Going home
Sometime tomorrow
To where it's better than before

Going home
Without my burden
Going home
Behind the curtain
Going home
Without the costume
That I wore.

Leonard Cohen
Going Home

Keep the Energy Flowing

Have you ever entered the home where an old person had lived and smelled that musty, stagnant smell that seems to sometimes linger around their clothes and other possessions? A musty smell is the sign of stagnant energies that can get stuck around objects, furniture and clothes. To keep everything fresh and energetically fluid it is important to not only clean one's home often, but also from time to time to clear out what no longer is being used, worn or read. Old clothes gather to themselves old energies, but as soon as they are washed and worn again, they become refreshed as the energy starts moving again. Just as physical objects that are not cleaned or renewed gather dust and become neglected, so do energies need revitalizing. Breathing new life into them makes sure they do not become stagnant and stale.

It is the same with old habits, old thoughts and old grievances. Harping back to old hurts prevents a person from engaging in the new. An older person can become fixed in their habits—visiting the same places, going on holidays to the same resorts, meeting the same people, cooking the same food. To keep vibrant and strong it is important to introduce new knowledge and new activities into one's life. Trying something new and above all, creating something new, brings excitement and inspiration into one's life. Creativity is a spring that never dries up and the more one creates, the more the rejuvinating spirit of the muse attends one. It is the best and quickest way to uplift one's spirits and bask in the energizing aura of renewed vigor.

What Do You Want?

The question "What to do you want?" is like an engine that ignites a life and stirs it into action. If there comes a point in one's life when that question is no longer considered, then the life and the energies that accompany it can become inactive and stagnant.

A person who wants nothing has no incentive to get up in the morning and to forage within the planet's energy realms for their next energetic food or fix. To want something or to want to be somebody or to want to do something is to be alive, to be human. We are made to have goals, ambitions, aims and wants.

As a person matures, their wants shift from desiring material possessions or from desiring another person to wanting success, recognition and fame. These wants are the hallmarks of the mid-life time when one becomes more aware of one's life's journey. It is the time when most people go through a thorough review of one's journey so far.

In the final stage of life the list of what one wants shifts again and what one usually desires above all else at this time of life is health and good experience for one's family and one's loved ones. At this age the center of gravity naturally shifts from oneself to others and then to the greater view of the planet. An older person has naturally a larger view and takes into consideration, when taking on a particular task, the legacy they are leaving behind.

I believe that knowing what you want is the first step towards making it happen. Declaring it reinforces the signal which is an invitation to receive the fulfillment of your desires. Writing it down is another reinforcement of your determination to make your dreams come true.

When I was working in Toronto, Canada, at a distance from home and in a job that I did not enjoy, I wrote down a list of what I wanted from a new job. I wanted it to have the following:

1. To be close to home.
2. To have a gym nearby so I would be able to exercise during my lunch hour.
3. To make more money.
4. To have a nice boss.
5. To work with a Mac instead of a PC.

I wrote down the list, contacted an employment agency and soon received a job offer where all my requirements were fulfilled. The gym was actually in the same building as the office! The one thing I forgot to ask was for the job to last. Within six months the department where I was working had been down-sized and I was out of my dream job. (It all ended well because together with my husband we decided to set up our own business. I never went to work for somebody else again!)

My mother-in-law used to always say that she wanted to die before her husband, my father-in-law, and she did. I intend to follow in her footsteps in this regard. My mother always used to say that she wished to die in her sleep and she did. I do not intend to follow in her footsteps in this regard. I believe we can magnetize the energies we desire to ourselves and achieve what we desire. We can certainly plan the way we wish to go when the time comes. I intend to be fully conscious so I can choose the thoughts and feelings I wish to connect to when the time comes.

HOW WANTS EVOLVE WITH AGE:

1. Possessions
2. Adventure
3. Sex
4. Relationships
5. Recognition
6. Wealth
7. Happiness
8. Success for others
9. Health
10. To leave a meaningful legacy

To Reincarnate or Not to Reincarnate

If you had the choice, would you want to reincarnate and do it all over again? It would mean being born, growing up, learning to read and write, making friends, building relationships, having sex, growing old. What if you had a choice and the opportunity of reincarnation depended on whether you believed it was possible or not and whether you wanted to reincarnate or not? Perhaps these two questions are worth addressing as you age. Even if you do not believe in reincarnation, it still might be worth considering whether you would want to, if such an opportunity presented itself to you.

Towards the end of life one might legitimately ask, "So what was it all about?" All the effort, the growing up years, the discovery of sex, building relationships, looking for satisfaction, trying to earn a living, having a family, establishing a career, travel and the desire for fame, wealth and prestige—what was it all for? And what about the planet's investment in us—the food, the water, the air and the energy—what was it all for and what was the planet's return on her investment? Was it all worthwhile? If asked, what would she say? Would she say, "I gladly provided him or her with food, drink and adventure, just to experience the fine energies he or she provided me with so I could grow and develop"?

How attached to the planet are you? Is reincarnation onto other planets in other solar systems possible? If so, trying to imagine one's future life can be a great exercise in developing one's imagination. I believe there is an intelligence inside us that knows about other worlds and other possibilities. We have embedded in us memories of other lives. Perhaps we just need to learn to listen...

Contemplation 2

Spend a moment considering the following question: if you died tomorrow and had the opportunity to reincarnate, where would you choose to be born? Who would you want to be your parents? Is it anyone you know? Would you choose to be rich or poor? What kind of home would you want to grow up in? Above all, would you want to do it all again? If there was a choice, would you prefer to reincarnate into the past, the present or the future? Which continent would you choose for the place of your birth? What country? What language would you like to speak? After you die, do you want to go to heaven? If so, what do you think heaven is like?

Would you prefer to reincarnate elsewhere in the universe? Perhaps into a more advanced society? If so, what would it be like?

This contemplation is designed to open one's mind and perception to the possibility of reincarnation and the many possible lives after death; not to become fixed on any one outcome but to remain open to the possibility of choice.

Contemplation 3

Sit down with a calculator and try to add up how much you have consumed throughout your life—consider the four foods we consume every day of our lives. As far as physical (earth) food is concerned, how many loaves of bread, chicken, cows, fish, goats, grains, vegetables and fruits have you eaten throughout your life? Considering liquids (water foods), how much water, tea, coffee, milk, wine and juice have you drunk? How much air have you inhaled? How much energy (fire food) have you used? All this has come from the planet and from the sun and they have supported each one of us throughout our lives, asking for nothing in return but providing a firm foundation for our every step. Should this not give us confidence to succeed and cause us to want to pay back for our many gifts?

Imagine a warehouse that would contain everything you have consumed in your life. Add to that the clothes that you have worn and now discarded as old, the books you have thrown out, the notebooks you have filled through your school years and afterwards, old furniture, records, papers, shoes, toothpaste, makeup, shampoo, soap, pens, pencils… The list is endless. How big a space would you need to fit everything you have ever used up? Can you even imagine the size of such a building or warehouse or stadium?

The fact of this investment by the planet into our lives says that our existence is important and that we are meant to repay the planet for this greatest of gifts in some way. Old age is the time to consider this debt and to find ways to pay back.

We cannot give back what we have consumed over the years. The planet does not understand human monetary currency; to her money is just paper, bits of metal and electrical blips on a computer screen. But she does understand energy, so the best way to repay the Earth for our existence is to provide her with fine energy—elevated thoughts, sublime emotions and powerful qualities like love, compassion and kindness.

I Am Leaving

I am leaving. I don't know when and I don't know how, but one thing I know for sure is that I am leaving. The day is coming to say goodbye and farewell. The world will go on without me, as if nothing had happened. And I will go on without it. The great enigma of what next beckons and intrigues me. How does one step out of time into timelessness? Yet the spirit knows, it knows the way; it has been here before. It is the guide and the usher, the light that shines in the darkness.

PRAYER

Oh spirit, guide me and wash away my regrets. They are nothing but temporary illusions that hinder my progress. Let me see each mistake and every experience as a learning that has made me wiser so that I can leave clean and ready to proceed.

Anna

Anna is my landlady. In 1941, when she was 14 years old she was taken from her home in Slovakia and sent to the Nazi concentration camp in Auschwitz, in occupied Poland. She spent the following four years in four different camps until she was liberated by the Americans at the end of the war. As I am writing this book she is 86 years old. Anna has maintained her sense of humor and joy of life throughout the years of hardship, emigrating from her native Czechoslovakia after the Russian occupation in 1948—first to Israel, then Canada and finally to the United States which is now her adopted home.

When my husband David and I moved in to Anna's house in Queens, New York, her grown-up children (a son and a daughter) commissioned me to write, edit and publish her story. In the process of preparing her memoir for publication, Anna told me about a poem she used to recite in the Auschwitz concentration camp. This poem has probably saved her life, as she would recite it for Elisabeth Volkenrath who was an SS guard who saved her several times from the gas chambers by hiding her among the packages in the camp mail room, where she worked.

Here are a couple of fragments from the poem which I translated for Anna's book. It was written by the Czech poet of German descent, Jiři Walker.

DYING

When I die, nothing in this world will change,
Just a few hearts will flutter
like the morning dew on the flowers
Thousands have died, thousands are dying with me,
thousands more will die,
No one who has been born will be able to avoid death.
Death I am not afraid of, death is not evil;
death is an integral part of life...

But in dying every man must be lonely and alone.
When I die, nothing will happen
and nothing will change in this world,
Only I will leave my misery behind
and I will transform away from all that.
Hopefully I will become a tree, perhaps a child,
perhaps a pile of stones.
I am not afraid of death, death is not evil;
death is an integral part of life.

Yiři Walker,
Czech poet
The poet was dying of tuberculosis at the age of 24 and wrote this poem to his girlfriend before he died.

Aging With Grace

When one reaches a certain age, say sixty or seventy, and looks back on one's life, one tries to make sense of what had gone on in the years. Even the actions, efforts, encounters and relationships that at one point seemed like a waste of time, in later years can indicate a pattern and perhaps even present themselves as mistakes that had led to a very positive change in behavior or way of thinking.

A woman who had married an abusive man might now see this as a lesson to be more discerning in her relationships. A man who had stayed in a dead end job where he was unable to earn a promotion and where his boss seemed to be always picking on him and blaming him for his own mistakes and shortcomings might finally realize his worth and decide to move on not only to a more lucrative job, but to one that gives him more satisfaction.

So our mistakes might be painful at the time but they are in fact the best possible lessons because they point to our weaknesses, revealing the need for improvement. A life well lived is a story of human development, full of failures and mistakes, leading to improvements and lessons learned, as well as victories and successes. While the body might grow weak and deteriorate, the spirit grows (or has the potential to grow) strong. We leave this planet carrying with us the light of the spirit and the difference between a well lived life and a squandered one is in how bright does the spirit become. It can be dim or incandescent—it all depends on how much light it has been fed and supplied with during the course of a lifetime.

If we can discover our own individual genius—whatever that might be—and develop it to the point where it gives us satisfaction and becomes the inspiration that drives us into new territories and adventures, then our life will become charmed. A person who lives with inspiration as a daily companion will radiate the light that will become attractive to others who want to share in their glory. If you ask someone, "What do you want to be?" and they reply, "What I am," they are indicating that they are connected to the inner life of the spirit. It is a sign of a person living within the glory of spiritual happiness.

It might take years to achieve this kind of satisfaction and to find the very thing that brings brightness, inspiration and a sense of accomplishment. Some people, like Mozart, know from an early age what they want to become, whereas others might spend a lifetime searching for that special something that inspires and drives a person to action and creativity. Sometimes there are early indications in childhood and it might be a good idea to look back to those years and to check what was it that had brought you joy as a child. A person's genius often shows itself in the early years, though it can then be overlaid and obscured with years of experience and the ongoing struggles to earn a living, bring up children and make ends meet.

But if a person decides to follow their chosen

path—whether they do so when still young or decide to make the necessary changes in later life—the path itself has a magical way of leading in the right direction. In other words, if one is doing what one was born to do, it will feel right and the next step will make itself known in due course. It is almost as if the journey is revealed one step at a time; the final destination remains unknown. But with trust and faith, it is like putting one foot in front of the other, always being watchful to see what might appear next.

Spiritual happiness does not descend on a life as soon as a person finds the special activity, art or calling they were born to achieve and follow. It is an ongoing process and as long as they pursue their dream, they will feel they are on the right path. The secret is to keep going and to believe that life is a purpose and a calling.

And even I own a plot of land,
as large as my bare foot can cover,
as long as I keep walking.

Cyprian Kamil Norwid
Polish poet
1821-1883

Sex and Old Age

One of the common fears associated with growing older is the lack or diminishment of the sex drive. Few books mention the "senior orgasm," or dare to estimate at what age it might diminish or disappear entirely.

If you believe that Creation is purposeful, then you must wonder why women who have passed through menopause still feel sexual urges. Clearly, the purpose of sex is not just procreation; it serves a far greater purpose. Sexual proximity causes intimacy between two people that is hard to achieve without it. The human touch causes the transference of energy from one person to another. It can be felt not only at the physical level; it brings sustenance to the emotions and feeds the soul as well. This exchange is very important in any relationship. It brings with it reassurance that all is well; it provides the warmth of an energetic exchange and is a healing that causes a glow from the inside out. When accompanied by love and respect between two people, this energetic illumination helps combat diseases, infections and other invasive influences that our modern environment is full of.

If one could see the exchange of energy that occurs during the act of sex or during any physical intimacy, one would be amazed at the fireworks and incandescent sparks that travel from one person to another. When two people are in close proximity with each other and sexually aroused, "sparks fly," even across a crowded room or a busy street. Sex is not a domain solely claimed by youth as their own; older people have their desires, too. Perhaps seniors are not as spontaneous as young people and are more discerning as to who they are attracted to and what they permit themselves to do, but sex is an important part of their lives. The energy of sex can keep a person younger longer and can bring invigoration and a renewed zest for life.

The same energy that is manufactured and exchanged during the act of sex also accompanies any creative endeavor. It is a vibrant green energy, that is also healing and invigorating. That is why when a person is inspired by what they create, they have energy to spare and can keep on going for long periods of time, sometimes without much food or drink. Inspiration is a powerful energy. When older people can follow their creative urges, they will most probably live to a very old age and bring satisfaction and well being to their days as they do so.

The Loneliness of Old Age

As one gets older, a strange sense of loneliness can grow upon a person, even when surrounded by family and friends. It comes with the realization that just as one was born alone, so one will die alone. At that final moment there can be no blame and no passing on of responsibility for one's actions, behavior and emotions to others. We are who we have become through the vicissitudes of life and we own it as we become it and it is what we find in the golden pot at the end of the rainbow.

The loneliness is a strength as well as a weakness. Just as no one else can take our place when we are due for a dental checkup or medical procedure, so the final farewell is a one man or one woman play. It can be our finest moment—the culmination of everything that has occurred through one's lifetime before. At the moment of departure a person has accumulated the most experience they will ever have and has lived through the largest number of days.

When contemplating one's future and the time one has left, one might wonder how many days, weeks, months and years there are remaining to live through. Of course, no one knows exactly how large or small that number is, though many might estimate. But one thing is certain—the number is finite. In fact it is already finite the moment a baby is born, but no one thinks about that because everyone who witnesses the birth of a baby is convinced that the child will outlive them, and therefore the child appears to be immortal to the parents and other adult members of the family. But our time here is limited and the realization that this is so can on the one hand become an excuse for resignation; on the other it can become a spur to action and an effective nudge to prepare for the culminating role one plays in one's own departure scene.

As one grows older, many friends and family members, as well as teachers, mentors, celebrities and role models pass away. More and more one is left to one's own devices. Life teaches us that being dependent on another person—whether financially, emotionally or intellectually—can lead to disastrous results. Other people might not be there for us when we need them (for whatever reason) and we might end up outliving them. It is the natural course of life that the older generation of parents and teachers should depart before we do.

There is an equation that can help in being fortified by the loneliness of old age, rather than becoming weakened by it. If one can substitute the word loneliness with the word solitude, one might learn to appreciate one's own company and become settled to moments alone. An older person who is their own best friend will enjoy many moments of contemplation, cherishing their time alone.

If one can become interested in one's own thought and internal processes, one needs never to be bored, lonely or feel abandoned by others.

Keeping the Memory Alive

It is generally believed that the memory diminishes with age. It is true that as we age, some of our brain cells die, but it has also been proven that brains can reorganize themselves so that as one cell dies, another one can take on its function. Memory is a faculty that has developed over the course of evolution and, as with every faculty, it is a question of "use it or lose it." It is also generally understood that older people on the whole remember well what had happened years ago when they were younger, but their short-term memory can become impaired.

It is a wise person who takes on precautionary steps to prevent memory loss. There are many books, CDs and courses that teach a person how to improve their memory. The old game of pairing cards that are turned face down is a good one; remembering a tray full of objects and then writing all the objects down after having looked at them for just a minute is another.

Association is a good way to remember shopping lists or a number of items. Take, for example, the following random list of ten objects:

pen
cigarette
button
envelope
scissors
fork

television set
car
house
tree

Now cover up the list and see how many you remember. Five? Six? All ten? Seven is a good result.

Now try this list of words rhyming with the numbers:

One is a bun
Two is a shoe
Three is a tree
Four is a door
Five is a hive
Six is a pair of sticks
Seven is heaven
Eight is a gate
Nine is a line
Ten is a hen.

How many did you remember? All ten? That is usually the answer.

So now let's use this list of rhyming objects to remember the first list. The brain remembers what is extraordinary, so let's put together some unusual images for you to remember. This will help you not only remember the list of objects but also the correct order they were written in.

Here goes:

Imagine a pen stuck in a bun.
Imagine a cigarette sticking out of a shoe.
Imagine a button hanging from a tree.
Imagine an envelope stuck in a door.
Imagine scissors being left on top of a hive.
Imagine a fork placed between two sticks.
Imagine a television set being watched in heaven by angels sitting on a cloud.
Imagine a car crashing into a gate.
Imagine a house with feet crossing a line.
Imagine a hen flying into a tree.

(Remember, we had a tree at number three, but this is number 10!)

Now see how many you remember. Ten? And you have just memorized two lists, not one! And you remembered the objects in the correct order!

Another way to remember is to create a story and to string objects together that way.

Here is another list:

Gnome
Cup
Statue
Jupiter
Lamp
Finger
Safety pin
Skirt
Soap
Water
Towel
Mountain.

Now let's weave an improbable story, bringing these objects together. The brain remembers what is unusual, so let's make the story out of the ordinary.

Once upon a time there was a gnome who lived in a cup. The cup was in an antique store and was displayed behind a statue representing the planet Jupiter. One day the gnome jumped out of his hiding place so fast that he knocked over a lamp. But he was strong and he was able to pick the lamp up with just one finger. He then went looking for a safety pin because he had torn his skirt. He found one but he pricked his finger and had to go to the bathroom to wash his hands with soap and water. While there he noticed there was a pile of dirty towels as high as a mountain.

How many did you remember? Did you notice that there were 12 objects on this list, not ten? And still, you probably remembered all of them.

Most people find it difficult to remember phone numbers. However, if you can find an association, the numbers are remembered more easily. Take, for example, this phone number:

(201) 700-7613.

It has the current year (2013) between which is sandwiched the year of the American Revolution with two zeros in the middle:

20......13

..17..76..

....00....

Now can you remember this number?

Here is another number:

(150) 074-1724

A little more difficult? Here is a sentence that might make it easier: One (1) James (five letters) Bond (007) with (four letters) a (one letter) license (seven letters) to (two letters) kill (four letters).

Now do you remember this number?

EXERCISE

Write down your own phone number, or a number you find yourself frequently dialing, and make up a sentence that will help you remember it.

Being a Witness

An older person is a witness to the cycles of life. He or she would have seen many children grow up, become adult and establish their own independent lives. We become the eyes of God as we hold in custodianship a bird's eye view of the entirety of human life.

It is an enigma why some people live to a ripe old age while others die young. Because there are fewer and fewer people in each consecutive age group as we grow older, those who survive the longest are in a way experiencing the changes around them and the revolving wheel of history on behalf of all those who have not managed to survive for so long.

Perhaps they are God's spies, and what they see is transmitted into the universe either in real time or when they pass over and take their memories with them. Perhaps their gifts harvested from this life are the energies they have accumulated in the way of sights, sounds, thoughts, feelings and experiences that they can take with them into the next life.

Memories

An older person will have witnessed many deaths. Perhaps not firsthand, but parents, friends and acquaintances will have by now passed away, leaving behind memories of times shared. Death is part of an older person's experience, something that is a repetitive reminder of one's own mortality.

The finality of death can haunt an older person. One can no longer say anything to someone who has departed; there is no more forgiveness and no more sharing of experiences and memories. As a person grows older one becomes the custodian of the stories of those who have departed and who can no longer pass on their own memories. As time goes by, there are fewer and fewer people who hold the memories of recent history from forty, fifty or sixty years ago.

For example, when the last person who was a veteran of World War One died, the live memories of those dark times died with them. The rest of us might remember movies or pictures we have seen, stories we have heard when younger from those who remembered those times. But live memory is different from hearsay. It carries an energetic charge that only someone who has witnessed an event can pass on and share with others.

Memories are precious. People who write about their lives, publish their memoirs and share with others their memories of times gone by do a great service to those generations that will come in the future. Their writings will help people understand the mentality that was prevalent in historic times and provide background to events that otherwise might seem impossible to believe.

Older people are witnesses to the revolving wheel of history. Their stories and memories are treasures that should not be dismissed or forgotten. Every person has a story (and many stories) to tell. If I could speak to all the older people in the world, I would encourage them to tell their stories and write their memoirs. In fact, I have helped several people publish their stories and will continue to do so as long as I am able to continue working.

DON'T STAND AT MY GRAVE AND CRY

Do not stand at my grave and weep

I am not there
I do not sleep

I am a thousand winds that blow
I am the diamond glints on snow

I am the sunlight on ripened grain
I am the gentle autumn rain

When you awaken in the morning's hush
I am the swift uplifting rush of quiet birds

In circled flight
I am the soft stars that shine at night

Do not stand at my grave and cry

I am not there
I did not die

Author Unknown

WHEN I DIE...

When I die—you will see me passing by
a look, a gesture, a wink of an eye—
I will be a migrating bird, high up in the sky
I will companion you when I die.

The immortal times we had and shared
are witness to the warmth and care
the live endearment we have had;
the times of being happy, sad.

So when we are gone and passed away
these holy substances will stay
to find a new stage on which to play
and gift another with a better day.

June 30, 2002

WHEN I DIE 2...

When I die there will be no more pain
no questions, no answers, no need to explain
unless reincarnation means I will come back again—
when I die there will be no more pain.

On Children

Your children are not your children.
They are the sons and daughters
of Life's longing for itself.
They come through you but not from you,
And though they are with you
yet they belong not to you.

You may give them your love but not your thoughts,
For they have their own thoughts.
You may house their bodies but not their souls,
For their souls dwell in the house of tomorrow,
which you cannot visit, not even in your dreams.
You may strive to be like them,
but seek not to make them like you.
For life goes not backward nor tarries with yesterday.

You are the bows from which your children
as living arrows are sent forth.
The archer sees the mark upon the path of the infinite,
and He bends you with His might
that His arrows may go swift and far.
Let your bending in the archer's hand be for gladness;
For even as He loves the arrow that flies,
so He loves also the bow that is stable.

On Children
Kahlil Gibran

When one is older, the children, if there are any, are grown-up and perhaps have children or even grandchildren of their own. They are independent and have their own lives. Although a parent will always see their offspring as their little boy or girl, they must also realize that the man or woman their children have turned out to be are no longer their responsibility.

To have children who have families of their own is a blessing, as an older person experiences the joys of bringing up children without the burden of responsibility for their wellbeing. If the children are married, the parents gain access to a whole new family of in-laws that might not be of their choosing but is a fact of life and can become a source of new friendships and new experiences.

Our children represent a younger generation. They will think differently, dress differently and behave differently. They will bring up their own children differently. It is not for us to judge them. We can give advice, support them and honestly reflect back to them how we see them to be; however, they are responsible for their own lives, their families, their careers and their own thoughts. As they have grown up in different times than their parents, they can teach the older generation about the times they live in from the standpoint of a younger person. They will have unique insights about the current age in which their parents are experiencing old age and might have lost contact with the essence and vagaries of youth, the changing fashions and the priorities of the younger generation.

Our children are our teachers. They can push us to the edge and bring us back again with the sweetest moments of sharing, vulnerability and appreciation. They indicate to us how the world has changed, and point to the future. They inherit the Earth, but not for long, as they in their turn will pass on to the next generation the responsibility of creating a new future.

Our children and grandchildren contain the oldest, most evolved genetic to be found on Earth. Genetically children are older than their parents. The concept of indigo children (developed in the 1970s by Nancy Ann Tappe and further developed by Jan Tober and Lee Carroll) and crystal children, born in the 1990s, suggests that there are among us a growing number of people with psychic powers and abilities. Time will tell if this is true, but if so, it will indicate that evolution is not finished and that the human race as a specie is still evolving.

Our children are a reminder that everything is in flux as the constant stream of humanity enters and exits this planet through the revolving door of life.

> *We are not responsible for how we find life on planet Earth when we are born, but we are partly responsible for how we leave it behind when we die.*

Life Is Not Over

Sometimes old people think their life is over and that they don't amount to much. But this is precisely the time when they have the most to offer. When people think they are no longer useful or when they are completely ignored by others, self-doubt can set in.

When the friends and other family members pass away, loneliness can set in. Parents are long gone and without the support and encouragement of loved ones and those who had been our rock for a lifetime of sharing, it might seem that nobody cares anymore what we think and have to say and what we do. But this is exactly the time to say it, to write a memoir and to share one's wisdom and experiences.

This is the time to remain connected. When a spouse dies and the other partner feels alone and no longer needed or wanted—this is the time to get busy, to go out and join a club, a mutual interest group or to learn something new. Thanks to the Internet there are many opportunities to become part of a group, as in *www.Meetup.com*, where one can meet like-minded people, rekindle interests that might have lain dormant for years or learn a new skill.

It is a choice to live life fully to the end. The body might be older and less capable, but the spiritual energy grows stronger with age. If we listen, we will hear it urging us to action and to become processors and transmitters of fine energies that can benefit the planet, the environment and all people we come into contact with.

One way to look at it is to see your life as a training for this moment. Today you have the most experience and learning you have ever had. Today you are ready and well prepared to face the next stage of your life. Today you are the youngest you will ever be. It might be challenging and it might be difficult, but you are in the unique position to be fully qualified for this next opportunity. These are your crowning years and it is up to you to transform them into your crowning glory!

The Young and the Old

There is a curious affinity between the young and the old. They are both close to the entrance and the exit, just moving through time in opposite directions. The child has come from somewhere and is still benefiting from its universal energy connections; the old person, if open to it, is anticipating his or her exit, with thoughts and wonderment about what is next.

Both the child and the old person are not involved in the "rat race" of earning a living and providing for a family. The child is still free to discover itself and its desires, abilities and character traits; the older person is free to contemplate his or her past and prepare for the future.

The very young and the very old are both sprinkled with stardust which reaches out from beyond this life and gives the baby and the old person an aura that says, "You are mine; you are connected to the Universe."

Try Something New

When I was 67 I decided to become a personal trainer and by the time I was 68 I was working in a gym, helping women become more fit and lose weight. Apart from earning some extra money, knowing that I was useful to others helped boost my self-esteem and self-image. This is important for older people who sometimes can feel ignored or that they have been shunted onto the sidelines of life.

As long as we are alive, we can learn and continue to develop. Life can still be a cornucopia of opportunity, if we let it. It is important to not become locked into the groove of the same old habits, the same old thoughts and the same old actions.

Sprinkle your day with new thoughts and learn something new. It will exercise your brain and give you a space within which new inspiration, new creativity and new adventures can reach you and claim you as their own.

Preparation

How do you prepare for the future?

1. Put your house in order—write a will and decide who gets what. Get rid of what you no longer need.
2. Decide what you still want to achieve.
3. Write your memoir.
4. Consider what you want to do in your next life (if you have one).
5. Tell your loved ones who are still alive how you feel about them.
6. Enjoy yourself—do what you love.
7. Practice your memory—memorize a favorite poem.
8. Do something you have never done before (prove to yourself you can).
9. Meditate upon the cycles of life

On Aging

A ten-year-old looks at the twenty-year-old and sees an adult who lives in a different world. A twenty-year-old looks at a thirty-year-old and sees someone who is definitely past it and over the hill. A thirty-year-old looks at a forty-year-old and sees someone past their prime, fixed, no longer young. A forty-year-old looks at a fifty-year-old and sees someone who is slowing down and no longer up to very much. A fifty-year-old looks at a sixty-year-year old and wonders about retirement and the need for survival in old age. A sixty-year-old looks at the seventy-year-old and wonders what it is like to be at death's door. A seventy-year-old looks at an eighty-year-old and wonders how they have managed to live so long. And yet, when we reach each of these ages ourselves, our perception changes.

Age is clearly a matter of comparison and relativity. As we grow older, youth stretches like an elastic, extending into our increasing years, to encompass at first twenty-five, then thirty and even thirty-five. A sixty-year-old might even call a forty-year-old parent of grown-up children young. Hence the saying that policemen and doctors seem to grow younger all the time. As time moves on, it seems to go faster and faster, perhaps because there is so little of it left.

Between the ages of ten and twenty, twenty and thirty, thirty and forty, forty and fifty, fifty and sixty,

sixty and seventy, seventy and eighty we are given ten years to get used to the idea that yes, we will inevitably enter the next decade and that the next decade is valid too and in fact quite livable. During each consecutive decade there is time for values to shift. For example, during the ten years between thirty and forty the emphasis shifts from physical appearance and sexual performance (first self) to a growing concern with family, relationships, a career and religion (second and third self). As a person grows older, their priorities tend to shift towards more permanent values. If they do not, a person can become devastated by the deterioration of the physical temple (body) that houses the spirit, soul and energy life.

Aging is a natural process and one of the benefits of being older is that an older person knows and appreciates the feelings of a younger person, having been there themselves. With development this experience can be called upon at will and used to communicate with a representative of the younger generation. If you have been to a place, you can picture it in your mind, imagine you are there and remember what it was like. If you haven't, you can only guess and work it out, but you can never really know for certain.

The 21st century Western culture, in its worship of youth, has taken the dignity out of aging and the grace out of growing old. No one wants to be old anymore; there is no honor in the fact of aging and the younger generations no longer cluster around to learn the wisdom of the old, acquired on their journey of life. These times have introduced the retirement home, the old age pensioners' homes, the senior citizens' apartment buildings, the retirement villages and golfing communities. The elders of the tribe used to be the wise ones, respected and listened to by all. Nowadays they are kept out of sight and in isolation, unless they are fortunate enough to continue to work or to look after the next generation—the young children of the family.

The collectively manufactured energy worlds, produced by all those who have grown old throughout the history of planet Earth, can be challenging to an older person, for they are full of insecurity and worry about aging. These concerns press in on a person, even if they think they are settled to the age they are They may be settled now to being, for example, forty, but are they prepared for and settled to being fifty, which is coming in ten years' time?

The only way to survive the business of getting older is to acquire a larger view which sees the impermanence of all things as part of Creation's plan. Can we be different from everything on Earth and expect to be immortal? We were not meant to stay the same age or live forever—we are on a journey from somewhere and we are going somewhere, too. If we view this life as but a short sojourn and small part of our life in the Universe, we can be glad of and interested in every stage of the journey, for each decade brings its own revelations and learnings and opens up new opportunities.

Ceremony

All transitions in life deserve a ceremony. A ceremony can be a private event or it can be witnessed by family and friends. As a person moves from one age to another, their entire internal and external landscape changes. An adolescent, for example, will be interested in completely different things than a young boy or girl of, say, six. Likewise, an old person might no longer be chasing fame and fortune, but they are intensely concerned about the legacy they will be leaving behind.

In marking these transitions, one is acknowledging change in a person's life. On a daily basis it is hard to tell when exactly a young girl becomes a woman or when a young boy becomes a man. Around the world and in many religions and tribal traditions there are many ways to celebrate these passages. It cannot be said that the person becomes adult on one particular day or that a girl becomes a grown woman the moment she starts menstruating. Ceremonies help in acknowledging the fact of the change. For example, a young boy's self-view will no doubt change after a Bar Mitzvah and from the time of the ceremony his friends, family and community will treat him differently, inviting him, for example, to events and celebrations organized for grown-ups only.

Ever since recorded history, in every civilization, every culture and everywhere in the world where people have lived together, there have been rites of passage. There is something very powerful in being witnessed by many eyes, brains and hearts. A ceremony that is witnessed lives on not only in the memories of the people who are going through the rite of passage themselves, but also in the minds of those who were there and witnessed it taking place. The very act of witnessing sanctifies the ceremony; the ceremony is watched not only by people but by the energies and essences present. From then on the ceremony becomes part of the energetic history of the place and the tribe. In many cultures around the world it is believed that a ceremony is witnessed by unseen powers and essences, whatever name is put to these unseen but nevertheless always present powers.

CEREMONY OF DEDICATION

This is a ceremony symbolizing the release from the grip of the material worlds and the unlocking of wisdom. It can be performed by symbolically cutting strings attached to cards with descriptions of qualities and activities that a person no longer wishes to embody or entertain.

Write on cards all the activities and qualities you no longer wish to be attached to and deliberately cut the strings. Imagine being released from the grip of such qualities as, for example, impatience, greed or selfishness. These cards can then be safely burnt and the ashes discarded.

Write on cards the qualities you would like to see continue to grow and develop in yourself and attach them to violet ribbons, which you can then pick up and hold in your hand, while you read over to yourself the names of the qualities and activities written on the cards. This can either be witnessed by others or performed in solitude.

The violet ribbons can be visualized, rather than physically there. However, the sense of sight can cause a more powerful and vivid memory that can be more effectively re-evoked in times to come, when it might be beneficial to remind oneself of promises made from self to self.

Soul Tribes

Older people do not suffer fools gladly. They have too little time left to use it up on nonsense. Besides, they can usually easily see through a person and detect their intentions; they can also more easily recognize a member of their soul tribe. By soul tribe I mean people who might be born in different places on the planet, have different skin colors and adhere to different faiths, but who still understand each other and have enough in common for the conversation and energy exchange to flow with ease. People who belong to these different soul tribes will be able to pick up where they left off, even if they had not seen each other for years. They will enjoy being in each other's company and will have shared references. Not much needs to be said, but the energy exchange will enhance both parties so that at the end of an encounter both will feel uplifted and energized, even if the subject of the conversation was a complaint or grievance.

Throughout a life many acquaintances, friendships and liaisons are made, but few accompany a person through their entire life. When a person moves, changes jobs or joins a different congregation or club, people drop away. Despite the fact that they often promise to keep in touch, they mostly don't. An older person will have experienced many such promises and will have become wistful at the prospect of making new friendships last. However, by the same token, they will value the people they do still have in their life and appreciate the times they are able to spend with them. Time is one commodity they have little to spare, so they will be careful how they spend it, but generous with it with those they feel close to and who make them feel wanted and loved.

Marriage

At the time of writing this book I have been married for 35 years. Having had a relationship of such longevity one experiences many shared moments which contribute to a growing endearment and appreciation of each other. An older person realizes that a life together has its end and that most probably one partner will die before the other; statistically it is mostly the woman who lives longer.

This makes a person appreciate their spouse even more, so that love grows even stronger through the years. A long, successful marriage is a source of warmth, joy and shared endearments.

A marriage that has endured for fifty years, or more, for example, and has been successful without becoming stale, stagnant or uninspiring, will have gone through many stages, with both partners changing on the way and developing into new people. Both partners will become older, wiser and with many shared experiences and beliefs. The exchange of energy between the two will produce a strong bond, with mutual understanding, and there will be many instances of clairvoyance and ESP between them, when one partner will know what the other is thinking before the other one speaks; often they will be able to accurately read each other's moods and thoughts.

As time moves on, a couple might even begin to look like each other and people who meet them will think they are brother and sister, rather than man and wife. This is because the frequent exchange of energy will have aggregated and condensed into matter—each partner will have become the custodian of the other's frequency. "You matter to me," they might say to each other and it will be true.

Researching One's Roots

"Have you noticed how people seem very interested in these family things when they get older? Sixty is when it starts. That is when they really want to know who were their parents' parents and the parents of those ones before them."

Alexander McCall Smith
The Miracle at Speedy Motors
Anchor Books, 2008; New York, New York.

Some aspects of who we are and who we have become are due to our genes. Some of our strengths as well as our weaknesses can be traced back to our parents, our grandparents and our ancestors. Who were these people? Who else are we related to? Knowing about our family tree might help explain some of our idiosyncrasies and peculiarities.

Family becomes more important as we grow older. They say that blood is thicker than water and sometimes it is, though sometimes it is not. However, knowing who one's relations are and keeping in touch with them can expand our family circle and give access to people we might otherwise never have met.

Researching our family tree is so much simpler these days with information available on the Internet. There are also sites which help a person build their family tree, like *www.ancestry.com*, *www.genealogy.com* and *www.familytreemaker.com*. School and college records, as well as birth registrations are also available on line. If you wish to be in touch with childhood friends, school mates or colleagues from businesses you were employed at when younger, you can search for them on *www.Facebook.com, www.Linkedin.com, www.MySpace.com* etc.

Another reason to research one's family history is to know who one will be meeting after the demise of the physical body, if the theory of the white light and the greeting by deceased family members and ancestors is true.

"If you'll be joining the ancestors, it's useful to know who the ancestors are before you meet them."

Alexander McCall Smith
The Miracle at Speedy Motors
Anchor Books, 2008; New York, New York.

William's Lessons

In the poem *You Are Old, Father William*, from *Alice's Adventures in Wonderland* Lewis Carroll describes a conversation between a father and a son, in which the son questions his old man about the various feats of endurance the senior performs. With his usual wit and vast imagination, Lewis Carroll presents an extreme image of the old man's antics. Here is an attempt at an interpretation of the dialogue.

YOU ARE OLD, FATHER WILLIAM

"You are old, Father William," the young man said,
"And your hair has become very white;
And yet you incessantly stand on your head—
Do you think, at your age, it is right?"

"In my youth," Father William replied to his son,
"I feared it might injure the brain;
But, now that I'm perfectly sure I have none,
Why, I do it again and again."

Charles Dodgson (the real name of Lewis Carroll) was a mathematician and a photographer as well as a writer. He had a great knowledge of and love for the English language. He often used anagrams and onomatopoeia in his writings. The name *William* anagrams to *I am Will* and sounds like *will I am*—

perhaps an indication as to the ingredient necessary if one wishes to develop into an active old age.

Although it is rather debatable whether an old man would indeed stand on his head, the first reply by Father William indicates that he has come to know himself and he has no illusions—he is convinced he has no brain. So the first two qualities this unusual old man displays are physical agility and self knowledge.

"You are old," said the youth, "as I mentioned before,
And have grown most uncommonly fat;
Yet you turned a back-somersault in at the door—
Pray, what is the reason of that?"

"In my youth," said the sage,
as he shook his grey locks,
"I kept all my limbs very supple
By the use of this ointment—one shilling the box—
Allow me to sell you a couple?"

It is very unlikely that an ointment can keep a person active and toned. Many might try to achieve supple limbs in this way and advertisers keep trying to sell us the pill, the cream or the drink that will give us energy and preserve our youth. But there is no substitute for exercising!

"You are old," said the youth,
"and your jaws are too weak
For anything tougher than suet;
Yet you finished the goose,
with the bones and the beak—
Pray, how did you manage to do it?"

"In my youth," said his father, "I took to the law,
And argued each case with my wife;
And the muscular strength, which it gave to my jaw,
Has lasted the rest of my life."

Arguing with his wife has given the old man the strength and healthy constitution to make it possible for him to eat just about anything. This can be interpreted as the result of a longterm relationship, due to the benefits of companionship. Arguing is an integral part of sharing one's life with someone over many years. Having another person with whom to discuss the day's events and air one's points of view might not necessarily affect the digestive system, but it will certainly exercise the mind.

"You are old," said the youth,
"one would hardly suppose
That your eye was as steady as ever;
Yet you balanced an eel on the end of your nose—
What made you so awfully clever?"

"I have answered three questions, and that is enough,"
Said his father, "don't give yourself airs!
Do you think I can listen all day to such stuff?
Be off, or I'll kick you downstairs!"

Lewis Carroll
Alice in Wonderland
W.W. Norton & Company, 1990. New York, New York.

Father William becomes impatient—he does not suffer fools gladly, even if it is his own son. He has answered three questions and that is enough. He has no more time to waste. It might be his son who is asking, but he still threatens him and refuses to continue the conversation.

To reiterate, the recipe for keeping young and active, according to Father William, is to:

1. Develop will
2. Know yourself
3. Exercise
4. Develop lasting relationships
5. Do not suffer fools gladly, even if they are your own children.

Contemplation 4
The Sweet Farewell

Look at your body as if you were going to have to say goodbye to it. After all, you will be leaving it behind when you go. So look at it as at an old friend that you will be saying goodbye to.

Look at your hands. Remember some of the things that your hands have done for you. Think of all the skills that your hands have mastered through the years of learning and beyond—playing sports, playing a musical instrument, writing, cooking, making things…

Look in the mirror and remember the face you used to have. Think of the many changes your face has gone through. See the wisdom in your eyes and the laughter as expressed in your laugh lines.

Think of the various photographs you have had taken over the years—the many moods, ages and expressions. Think of all those yous and gather them together in your mind to join you in the here and now.

Find a way to express your gratitude. Your body will end up becoming part of the planet again, while you will be going on to your next life. Your body has been your friend, your servant and your teacher for many years, but there will come a time when you will have to leave it behind. Contemplate this fact and be grateful for the facility you have been given.

Relentless

Time is relentless. It keeps moving on. The only way to keep up with it is to keep moving on as well. Otherwise one can be left behind. As much as we might want to shout, "Stop, give me a break," or wish to add another hour to the day or day to the week, we know it is not going to happen. Tomorrow is on its way now and will assuredly, inevitably come. The seeds of tomorrow are sown today.

> *No matter how distant the future, it is on its way now.*

Be Healthy, Be Happy

In order to be happy in one's old age and to be able to pursue one's goals, one needs to be healthy. The health of the physical body is a priority and a foundation for the health of the spirit and for spiritual happiness to be possible. Physical health, wellbeing and fitness are not the object of this book—many writings already exist on the subject, recommending diet, nutritional choices, exercise routines and healthy lifestyles.

This book is about the energetic process of growing older and how an older person can become a beacon of hope and an inspirational role model for the younger generations following in his or her footsteps. It is about living a purposeful life in the light of the spirit, right until the time of exit, and enjoying being a wise, important member of one's community.

The Crowning Years

Violet is the crown wheel of energy (chakra), which is the seat of the connection to spiritual worlds and the highest energy available to humans on planet Earth. It represents connection to the divine and the opening of extra sensory capabilities, like ESP, clairvoyance and telepathy. It is very rare to see a person with a fully developed violet energy wheel, but if you should meet such a person, they would impress you with a sense of peace and serenity surrounding them; they would also embody such qualities as patience, humility, honesty and compassion. Both people and animals would feel their enlightened energy and want to be around them, so unless they were living the life of a recluse, such a person would be surrounded by people who would want to learn how to obtain what they had already achieved by their development.

If life can be likened to a journey through the chakras, wherein each wheel of energy becomes activated and developed at each stage, then the crowning years would be the time when the crown opens to higher influences.

If you rearrange the letters of the word *violet*, you get the anagram *love it* or *to live,* which describes exactly the opportunity of this time of life. It is a time of appreciation for all the people, situations and activities that a person had enjoyed and is still able to enjoy during their lifetime. According to spiritual traditions, it is potentially a time of looking back with gratitude and looking forward with expectation.

A life is coming full circle, approaching a new birth and a new opportunity. The seventh stage is the last one, but it can be much longer than 11 years, as there is so much that can still happen in a life after the age of 77, having gone through seven stages of 11 years' duration each. If a person wants to live a long life, they need to project beyond the age they hope to achieve, because longevity is a gifting of these times, at least in the Western world, and it is available to us, especially to the female gender. The author knew someone who wanted to live until he was 100 and because he never projected beyond that age, he died within months of his 100th birthday.

It is very clear that God or Creation wanted women to live beyond their child bearing years, otherwise we would die at menopause. In fact, menopause, at least for some women, might come just halfway through their lives. Therefore it is clear that having children cannot be the only purpose for which women were put here on planet Earth. If we live on average until 85, then child bearing and rearing takes up probably less than a quarter of our lives. So to identify one's significance solely with being a mother, family provider and nurturer must be a folly.

The seventh stage is the ultimate liberation. It is the time of retirement for most, when a person has the possibility of filling their time with what they want to do, no longer obliged to go to work every day and to help win the family's daily bread. This is the time to really begin to prepare for one's future life, the one that awaits beyond this one. As the time of departure draws near, we have little time to waste and to worry about small, insignificant matters.

This is a time of magnification—the magnification of value and importance that one has attached throughout life to events, people and activities. So as many things fall away and are no longer taken into consideration on a daily basis, others grow in significance.

Take, for example, relationships, either within the family, or friendships built through years of sharing time and experience with others. Some attachments might have endured throughout life, from childhood until old age, and as time passes, these relationships can deepen and grow. Thus if a person has witnessed the struggles, joys and adventures of another throughout their life, then the bonds between them will be very strong, with the continuous passage of energy from one to the other. As energy is exchanged between people, it is accompanied by a small amount of matter that grows over years. This is why people who spend a lot of time together, especially if that time is emotionally charged, begin to look like each other. Sometimes pet owners will eventually begin to look like their pets as well.

As men live shorter lives than women, this can also be the time of widowhood when grief takes its toll and a woman needs to adjust to living on her own, after perhaps many years of a shared life. Therefore it is important that a woman is never totally dependent on a man, either financially or emotionally, and always maintains her own interests and connections, because she will often need to be able to survive beyond the shared life she had known with her husband or companion.

As a person becomes a widow or widower, so they will need to deal with their grief, which is a natural response to the loss of a loved one. Having lived together for many years, the exchange of energy that has gone on on a daily basis abruptly comes to an end. When a person dies, that energy, which had been lodged in the other person over the years, returns to them, which is the source of its arising, to accompany them on their next journey. Therefore when someone dies, it is best to consciously release the energy that belongs to them and let it go, rather than holding on and wishing they were still alive.

As some faculties do deteriorate with age, it is vital to keep as active as possible, exercising one's mental and physical abilities, so as not to fall prey to the law of "use it or lose it." There is a story of a convent in the United States, where the nuns are mostly old—in their seventies and eighties—but very active and mentally agile. None of them seem to suffer from Alzheimer's or any other mentally debilitating disease. This was such a phenomenon that these nuns were studied by specialists and consequently became known for their longevity and health. It turns out that they practice mental exercises daily and are very active in many ways, all participating in the running of the convent. They also have the support and companionship of each other, where there is a sense of camaraderie, which has no doubt helped them maintain continuous health. The fact that they have a defined mission and a dedication, so that their faith keeps them strong and united, is also an important contributory factor to their longevity and health.

Thus it is important at this time to maintain one's sense of mission and to keep alive one's dedication, interests and commitment to a cause. It is also a time of putting one's house in order, in preparation for departure from this earthly journey to begin the next phase of one's existence.

The Spiritual Journey

A person's spiritual dedication undoubtedly supports the maintenance of their overall health, especially in later years, when the attachment to material possessions wanes. At this time in life a person realizes that they are here on planet Earth for a limited time and that the acquisition of wealth does not count for much in the long run.

We are all visitors here, and very temporary visitors at that, whose life runs out so very quickly. You cannot say this to a young person (though many try), as young people will always think they are immortal and that their youth is a perennial gift from Creation, even though the evidence of their eyes and elders tells them otherwise. It is only in the middle years that a person begins to seriously consider their mortality, and in later life this becomes a certainty—we are all going to die. A hundred years from now no one reading this book will be here any more and whole new generations will have grown up and taken over. All we possess will have gone onto the garbage heaps of tomorrow or will be inherited by our children or beneficiaries. Thus most traces of our life and signposts of our passing will have disappeared and even those who will grieve for us at our funeral will have passed away or will be getting close to the exit.

But while we are here we can still be of some account and help those who come after us to learn from our experience and wisdom.

Spiritually this is a time of preparation for the life yet to come. We do not know where we are going or what will happen to us when we die, but everything we experience in our life and all our researches must give us some indication in a conscious way that there is life after death and that our existence is a continuum. The spirit knows for certain, for it is immortal and it is going home, wherever home happens to be. If we listen to the internal guidance of our intuition, we will hear the voice of the spirit, for this is the medium through which our spirit talks to us and guides us.

PRAYER

Give me the ability and strength to prepare wisely for my life to come. May I be sensitive and open to the call of the spirit as it instructs me and tells me what I still need to do before I am ready to depart this earthly plane.

Contemplation 5

Think of all the things you love to do. Imagine silver threads connecting you to these activities and as you do so, see how they grow in strength and radiate and shine.

Imagine that you are surrounded by the people you love and value and that there is a violet glow radiating from you and enveloping them as well. This is you at your best, because we are always at best when we enjoy what we do and are with those we love and respect.

Imagine the violet glow growing to encompass you, your loved ones and all those activities that bring joy and inspiration to your life.

Aging Gratefully

The seven ages of life can be likened to a journey through seven different bands of energy corresponding with the seven rainbow colors. Our lives change dramatically as we age and this process can be likened to a journey through bands of different colored energies—from red to violet, with three extra parts—the life in the womb (white), the entrance called birth (silver) and the process of dying (gold).

Throughout our life we are connected to unseen influences, which manifest in the form of energy, feelings, intuition and knowings. People who are especially susceptible to these multiple subtle influences will instinctively respond to the changing seasons of their life. They will feel their energy adjusting to each stage of life and they will embrace these changes as they learn to make the most of each age they go through. This alternative view of the art of living and dying, which takes into account the changing energy of each stage of life, can help a person in managing not only their day to day living, but also in achieving long term aims and goals. If we knew when we were six that we would no longer be interested in toys by the time we were sixteen, would we have placed such value on each one of them? Or if a girl understood that menstruation gets less painful and cumbersome as she gets older, perhaps she wouldn't mind the pain so much. And if a boy knew that he would learn about his body and his needs as he grew older, he might have a bit more patience as a youngster to give himself time to prove to himself his sexual prowess.

The human passage from childhood to adulthood and into old age is marked by definite events and once they have occurred, everything in a life changes and there is no going back. So, for example, when a girl begins to menstruate, in many cultures she is from then on considered a woman and no longer a child. One day she goes to bed firmly based in her childhood and the next night when she rests to her nightly slumber, she is a woman. Accompanied by ancient rites of passage, this would have been a momentous event, but today it usually goes by unnoticed by others, though for the girl herself it will still be an important experience that she will no doubt mention to her mother or friends. Likewise, once a boy's voice breaks or he starts to need a shave every morning, he will be treated differently by all who encounter him.

Throughout life we go through seven ages, but not all of the seven stages are separated by such distinct markings as the beginning of menstruation, the growth of a new set of teeth or menopause. However, each stage marks remarkable change that every person alive goes through on their journey from birth to death. However young or old a person looks, however young or old they feel, however many plastic surgeries they might have gone through to conceal their age and stop the encroaching march of time, time does move on. If only we could learn to befriend the process of aging, and to welcome the changes our minds, bodies and personalities go through and work with them, rather than against them, our lives would be so much richer, rewarding and real.

Life experience is a gifting, an invitation to join and enjoy the exploration of the changing scenery of our lives. It is an encouragement to learn to love every moment as it passes by, for we will never be able to live this moment again. All our experiences are given to us to learn from and they were all put in place to give us the necessary development to successfully make the next major transition we are all heading towards, which is death or departure. If we can see death as a gateway to our new life, then perhaps it will cease being a frightening specter looming at the end of the journey, but rather a welcome and anticipated changing post where a new life begins.

We are so used to the connotation of the words *birth* and *death* that automatically we attach a feeling and an instinctive reaction to both. The word *birth* brings with it an image of a new life beginning, causing joy, happiness, expectation. It brings to mind rosy cheeks and big shiny eyes, toothless gums and the sounds of gurgling—all the paraphernalia of a new baby appearing on planet Earth. It is an event that will be henceforth celebrated every year by family and friends, always marked down as an important identification, whether by authorities who issue our passports, driving licenses and birth certificates, or by astrologers who divine our future and our potential according to the layout of the planets and stars at the time of birth. Never again will the heavens be exactly configured as they were when we were born and although other babies might have arrived at exactly the same time as we had, they were not born in exactly the same place. Their horoscope would be minutely or even quite dramatically different if, for example, they were born on the other side of the world, twelve hours earlier or later (though at the same time in real time). Curiously enough, a baby born in New Zealand hours later than a baby born in Europe might actually have an earlier year written on their birth certificate if they were born before midnight on December 31st. So according to the year of their birth they will be a year older than their European counterpart and consequently might end up in a class above the European child if they go to the same school, even though in real time they will always be the younger of the two.

Death, on the other hand, brings images of funerals, grieving, sadness and sorrow. In the West we wear black as a mark of respect towards the deceased and their family, we sympathize with those who are left behind and attend the funeral of the deceased to say our final goodbyes. We then spend time remembering the deceased as they were during their lifetime, recalling the good times and their best qualities, in an attempt to preserve the best memories we associate with them. Death has a sense of finality about it, and it brings us face to face with our own mortality; it is a reminder of what is to come to us all.

Here is a suggestion, how we can begin to think about these two opening and closing chapters of our life on planet Earth—marked in the society we live in by the words *birth* and *death*. What would happen if we reversed these two words and began thinking of our arrival as a death, because, after all, we did come from somewhere and had to die to that place in order to be born here? And what if we substituted the word *birth* for the word *death* and began to think of our earthly departure as being born elsewhere? For our life is going somewhere and although this book is not promoting any particular religion or belief, it is suggesting that as energy cannot be destroyed, so our energy life must go somewhere and when it arrives at its next destination, that will be its new birth.

In a hundred years from now none of our current family members or friends will be here and the world (if the human race does not destroy itself first) will be filled with new faces, new ideas, new fashions and new ambitions. All we have lived for will be gone and passed on, embedded in the works we had performed and the edifices we had created. As embodied forms of energy we are immortal, but our bodies do die and decompose. It is good sometimes to remember the brevity of our sojourn here, for this awareness helps put into perspective our temporary worries, stresses and difficulties.

Most people view their life as open-ended—it has begun, but is not going to end; it is a continuum of mornings, afternoons and evenings with subtle shocks when the biological clock strikes forty, fifty or sixty years old. These shocks are then overcome by pushing the barrier designating old age higher and higher, so that at twenty, thirty seems old; at thirty it moves to forty, and at forty to fifty. We always seem to be at least a decade away from old age. But what happens when it has nowhere to move to? That is the time when we look in the mirror and face it head on. We are old; people start treating us differently and there is no further place to hide.

Aging is said to begin around eleven. In its first stage (red) the baby and child grow stronger and more self-sufficient until it reaches the turning point at eleven, as it enters the second stage (orange). Before eleven a child is less likely to die with each passing year. After eleven, statistically speaking, a person is more likely to die with each passing year. In the industrialized West the risk of dying then doubles every eight years. Women live longer than men and are less likely to die at any given age than their male counterparts. The female is better designed for survival. Another aspect in considering this statistic is the increased risk of men dying from puberty to thirty, caused by accidents, war and violence, i.e. aspects of human behavior that affect women far less than men, and are not natural causes of death.

We are told that in order to have a good and productive life, it is important to love life and to live life to the full. That is what we are supposed to be doing here on planet Earth. The quality of our life after death depends on what we do with this one and how we manage and use up all the gifts or talents we were given at birth. However attached we might be to our daily experiences, they are all transitory and passing by so quickly. It is almost as though the moment we become attached to a feeling, an experience, a person or situation, the moment we decide we are comfortable with how we feel about ourselves and the age that we are, it passes. As one stage passes, the next stage of our journey immediately follows and then yet again we have to adjust and adapt to this new shift in energy alignment. This is not a planet of comfortability and although it may seem that there are people here who lead comfortable lives, this is not so, for even the most comfortable and satisfying moment will pass and the next fleeting moment will urge us to recapture that sensation and relive it again. This, of course, is an impossibility because every satisfaction, joy or sorrow is different, as time moves on. New experiences await us as our energy continues to evolve and change and life surprises us with ever renewing sensations, feelings and discoveries.

Throughout our lives we process two kinds of energy—the vigor of youth which begins to wane around our mid twenties, and the wisdom and spiritual resilience of the older years, which begins to take hold, if we are open to it, around the mid-life stage. Just as the physical energy has its definite increase and decrease, as well as its continuing decline, so the spiritual vigor continues to rise, becoming potentially prominent and influential in the second part of life. The changeover from one form of energy to the other is a crucial time as far as aging gratefully is concerned. If a person can be firm in their belief and their self-belief by this time, then they will be able to see clearly the way ahead, rather than fear the years to come. This changeover is a time to consider such issues as security, planning for one's old age and taking care of physical health, in the pursuit of wellbeing and longevity.

In our society youth is glorified and as a result

of this distorted image, most people want to remain younger longer. If this were not the case, then there would never be such a market for anti-aging cream, hair color and transplants, botox and plastic surgery. But all these items and services do very well and continue to prosper. What would it be like if we never saw our face? After all, we cannot see it through our eyes and we need the assistance of the reflection in a mirror, a photograph or the reaction of another person to know what we look like. What if we didn't have these external reflections? Do women put makeup on when they spend a day at home alone? Do men dress up in a suit? And why do women apply hair color containing chemicals, which they know are not good for them, just to look younger? If our society respected their old folk, like many indigenous people do, and wanted to hear their wisdoms and stories about their ancestors, then perhaps old people would become proud of being old and wear their graying hairs and wrinkles like a badge of honor, gained with valor through the years. Simply by successfully living through all seven stages, a person inevitably acquires experience and learns by their mistakes. If they had a forum within which to share this wisdom with others, there would definitely be fewer people suffering from the diseases of old age, which no doubt are in part caused by a lack of direction or purpose and the fact that there is no audience to talk to. Living in an old folks' home and sharing their time mostly with other old people who mostly have similar stories to tell is not a very inspiring circumstance within which to practice one's art of sharing.

It makes so much more sense for old people to live within the community, to become the elders that others look up to and seek guidance from. And although old people do not move with the times at the increasing pace at which the younger generations seem to be galloping forward from ideals to ideas, they still have a lot to offer. They are the historians and pioneers of their age, who in their time were the rebels against the prudery and limitations of their elders.

With every generation new children appear, as the youth of yesterday ages and become parents, ushering in the young. Always the children are yet again connected in to the incredible vigor of youth, the supply of which never seems to decrease or wane. It is a miracle of Creation engineering that this universal allowance continues unabated, to the inspiration of all who perceive it. The human race continues, despite hardships, pollution, diseases, wars and other calamities, both natural and unnatural. Life springs eternal, as if it were never going to stop.

The repetitious nature of this unending cycle must bring hope to the human mind and heart, demonstrating that God and nature are on our side, fuelling the urge to continue and grow. As the generations come and go, and as one set of humans age, die and are replaced by another, it speaks of continuance and provides evidence that we too will live on.

It is the natural order of things that a seed planted in the spring grows throughout the season and sheds its foliage in the fall, only to fertilize and nurture next year's growth. And so it is the duty and privilege of this generation to ensure that the next crop of humans have a rich soil within which to plant their seeds.

The only way to a happy and productive old age, according to the author, is to fully embrace it and make the most of it while it lasts. Even the pain and difficulties are experiences that can add to one's knowledge and history. How we handle each obstacle on our path will become part of our toolkit and preparation for the life yet to come, an experience which we will take with us when we die. If we can see ourselves as the guardians of the spirit of the age and take this time of life—old age—to pass the torch of wisdom to the next generation, we will have served an important purpose and played our part well in the drama or tragic-comedy that we call life on Earth.

Further description of the seven ages can be found in my book, *Seven Ages of Woman, Kora Press, 2006; New York, New York.*

Available from *www.EnergyWorlds.com, www.KoraPress.com* and other on line bookstores.

The End Is Nigh

Death is when we achieve the pot of gold at the end of the rainbow. Every day you take a step through one of the seven energy bands closer to departure. No matter how young you are or how old you are, tomorrow you will have fewer days left to live. These last two sentences should not cause worry or depression, because death is not the end, as you may have been led to believe, but a continuance into the next stage of the journey and a release from planetary pain and suffering. Ask anyone who has had a near-death-experience (NDE) or out-of-body-experience (OOBE) and most probably they will tell you that they did not want to come back, but did so because they had some duty or tasking to complete, like looking after their children or fulfilling their life's mission. If we really knew and appreciated what awaits us on the other side of death, we would every night sigh with relief that yet another day has gone by that we do not have to live through again, no matter how good it was.

On the way to death there are many small deaths, as we bid farewell to childhood, then adolescence, then youth and in turn to each passing stage. As we say goodbye to one stage, we enter another, like going through a sequence of rooms in a house, where we move from the nursery to the play room, to the school room, to the study and so on… A person can look backwards with regret and wish for more time in the nursery, or they can wholeheartedly embrace the room they are moving into, marveling at the scenery and wishing to explore every nook, cranny and décor with curiosity and alacrity. The choice is up to each person and may have far reaching results, causing a life to be fulfilled and satisfied or always yearning for something that is no longer there.

The manner of our death depends on the manner of our life and there is strong evidence to support the idea that we can choose the way of our own departure. If a person knows what they want and knows how they want to die, then this can become their reality. There are many stories of people who knew in advance the time and method of their death, who therefore had time to plan for it and expect it. If it is possible for shamans, ancient Egyptian priests and Tibetan monks to know about death and dying, then this knowledge is also available to us in our time, when there are so many writings and researches available on the subject.

It is time we stopped ignoring the fact of death and sweeping it under the carpet, as if it really did not happen, or as if it was a disease or something gone terribly wrong. Death is the most natural and only conclusion to life on planet Earth and when approached with dignity and reverence, it can be the most uplifting experience of all. This is the final ceremony and the crowning event of our life. It makes sense to want to die well and with dignity, to be surrounded by those people that a person was close to in life. It makes sense to be able to say one's final goodbyes and to pass on any final words of wisdom, or to conclude any unfinished business one might have that is still outstanding.

They say that "you can't take it with you when you go," but there are energies and qualities that do accompany a person during their final moments on Earth. Throughout a lifetime of experience a wise person will have accumulated many qualities within their aura or energy field. Unlike their material possessions, these will ease their passage and help in the next transition as they reach "the end of the rainbow."

People tend to speak of the departed as of the "lost." But perhaps they are indeed found. Memories of them remain with those who are still alive and if they are remembered well and they have left a legacy behind, then the world will be a better place for having been host to them.

PRAYER

May I remember to be grateful for my life and all the special gifts that have been my privilege to receive. I wish to take with me the best of myself and the best of my experience to help me on the way. May I view my life as an interim sojourn in preparation for the next stage of my journey, whatever that might turn out to be.

Contemplation 6

Imagine that you are old and you realize that the time for your next birth is approaching. Ask yourself, what would you want to have achieved by the time you are, say, eighty or even ninety. Think of all the things that you have already done in your life and project that into the future. Write down your wishes and look at them often. You might find that you need to adjust your projections as the years go by, so this could be an ongoing meditation, repeated, say, once a year, perhaps at the time of the New Year.

Ceremony 2

This is a time when a person is summing up their life and preparing for departure. It is important to leave behind those aspects which are no longer energizing and to embrace all that has been of quality. This could be performed as a gathering with friends and family who are able to help a person remember the good times, to cherish fond memories and to reflect a person's best qualities back to them, so that they can be reinforced in their best view of themselves. A bit like a wake before death, it will arm a person with the necessary strength to support them on their journey through the next gate, or the birthing into what is next.

Forgiveness

On a warm day in September 1975 at the age of 32 I was standing in the foyer of the Hilton Hotel in London, making a phone call from one of their soundproof booths, when a bomb detonated in the middle of the lobby. My back was turned to the explosion and the sound was muffled where I stood, so I did not know what was happening and I thought it was something wrong with the phone, as I could see sparks flying and my connection went dead. My left arm was resting on a ledge where I had placed my bag and at first I did not even realize that I was hurt. As I slowly turned around I could see a small fire burning in the middle of the lobby, someone was lying on the floor and a man was running towards me. As he escorted me out of the building, I began to realize that I must have been injured. I could hardly breathe and all I could think of at that moment was my next breath.

I had gone into the Hilton Hotel at Hyde Park corner to make a phone call. I had taken a bus from the apartment where I was living at the time above an antique shop in the trendy Kings Road, Chelsea. It was the last day of my holidays and I was due to return to work at the Performing Right Society in the West End the next day. I was enjoying this last day of leisure, having safely escorted my son Peter to an English school. After a year of establishing myself in Britain, in a new job and applying for a British passport, I had at last been able to bring my son to live with me in my new country. I had just returned to England from Poland, where I grew up and where my son was born. Three days earlier we had arrived at Victoria station, and I was explaining to the five-year-old boy that he would need to learn a new language, as not many people in London spoke Polish. We caught a taxi from the station to the apartment and on the way I was telling him that he would not be understood, when the taxi driver turned around and started speaking fluent Polish to us.

On the previous day Peter had gone to school for the first time in his young life and he began by learning English in a special class for foreign students. He had been quite upset that he was not in class with the other children and again, I explained to him that he needed to learn the language first before he could rejoin the regular lessons. So on this particular day I had taken him to school and was on my way to meet a girlfriend for lunch. I had tried to phone her from the phone booths at Sloane Square, as this was a time before the Internet and cell phones. All the phone booths that I tried were either occupied or not working. In the meantime a bus came along and I jumped aboard, planning to phone from the Hilton Hotel, where I knew there were several public telephones in the lobby.

So there I was, being escorted to an ambulance which was taking a number of the people from the hotel who were injured to the nearby hospital of St. Michael's which at the time was located at Hyde Park Corner. I learned later that my arm was badly hurt and I was very lucky that there was a visiting surgeon from Australia who specialized in skin grafts, for I needed both skin and bone transplants. The doctors debated whether to amputate my arm, but decided to perform the necessary operations to save it, because the nerve connections were intact and I still responded to stimuli to my left hand. So six operations later, I now have skin from my abdominal area on my arm and skin from my leg patching up my abdomen. I have a piece of my left hip bone inserted into my lower arm as well as a metal plate. However, I feel whole and I am grateful to have two working arms and two legs, even if one limb is somewhat disfigured. I feel very grateful to be alive, for if I had stood a few inches further left, it could have been my head that was hit, not my arm.

I took several lessons from this experience. One is that anything can happen any time, and no matter how well you are prepared or think you are prepared for life's offerings, there are always surprises—both good and bad. Even the "bad" ones have good lessons to offer, because difficult experiences are character forming and strengthening. I believe that those who have been through life's turmoils and tribulations are better equipped to extend a helping hand to others in need.

A few weeks later, when I was still in hospital, the evening news came over the radio and there was an announcement that there was another bombing nearby, at Green Park. I was very moved to watch dozens of doctors and nurses streaming back into the hospital, because they had heard the news on their way home and had turned around in case their help was needed. Luckily, not many people were hurt this time. But the feeling of community, solidarity and humanity constituted a very healing presence in the hospital that night.

When in hospital I wrote the following words:

THERE IS A PAIN

There is a pain beyond which there is no pain
There is a fear beyond which there is no fear
There is a belief beyond which there are no doubts
And I will have the strength to reach it.

The IRA (Irish Republican Army) claimed responsibility for the bombing in the Hilton Hotel that day. After the incident, when this fact became known, people would ask me, "Aren't you angry?" or, "Don't you want revenge?" or, "Doesn't it make you feel bitter?" My reply to them was, no, I do not want to take anger or bitterness or hate into my life. People who plant bombs do so out of hate. If my response was hate, then I would become like them, taking the very disease they suffer from into myself. People who feel hatred and harm others will need to live with the fact that their life is about hate and anger. My life is not about hate and anger; it is about forgiveness and learning and helping others. How can I improve if I want revenge? I am not responsible for other people's lives, but I am responsible for mine. So today I feel that if I can pass on this one lesson that I have learned, then I will have made good use of the experience on that fateful day, difficult as it was at the time.

As for my son, some good and generous people that I worked with took care of him and by the end of six weeks, when I came out of hospital, he spoke English quite well!

Two Healings

When I was in my fifties I fell downstairs and broke my shoulder. I needed surgery and now I have some screws and wire keeping my shoulder in place. During the convalescent period my husband and I visited some friends in a small village in the Galilee in Israel, called Ma'ale Tzvia. In that village they have a Healing Garden and I was invited to sit for a while within its healing presence. On the first day, while sitting and quietly meditating, I had a revelation: a voice in my head told me that I needed two healings, not one.

The first healing was the healing of the injury itself—a broken shoulder takes time to heal. The second injury was mental and emotional—I needed to forgive myself for falling down the stairs. It wasn't until that moment that I realized how I had blamed myself for not paying attention and for falling down. Stairs are indeed dangerous and these days I am very careful when walking downstairs. But once the damage was done, it was time to heal and to forgive myself for causing the injury.

I think the need for two healings applies to most hurts, illnesses and diseases, especially when we are the cause of our own injuries. We need to learn to forgive ourselves because forgiveness is the balm that will allow a healing energy to support us in the natural healing process.

Afterword

I love being old. As long as I am healthy and mentally alert, I think it is a great age to be. I am the wisest I have ever been and with the most experience—I have weathered change and survived the vicissitudes of the many stages of life. My son is grown up now and responsible for his own life and that of his family. Although I still worry about him and he will always be my little/big boy, I no longer cook for him, buy him clothes and physically care for him on a day to day basis.

I am experienced in my work and I have the great fortune to be able to do what I love and be paid for it. My relationship with my husband David has survived and flourished for 35 years and in that time we have shared many endearments and experiences that have built a rock solid foundation of friendship, love and support.

I am part of a community of like-minded people who are spiritually aware and contributing to the culture of personal development and growth. I believe there is a growing personal development movement in the world and a new influx of energy from the Universe, encouraging the human race to become more conscious and to take up the tasking of becoming responsible stewards of the planet, the environment, the future and our own lives.

I am also grateful in the knowledge that if a man speaks to me, I no longer have to wonder whether it is in fact sex that he is after rather than being interested in me as a person.

There are other fringe benefits to the fact of being a senior. Sometimes I even get offered a seat on the subway. Movie tickets are cheaper and some stores offer me special discounts. I receive a small pension from three governments and I have time to pursue my chosen path.

I am the youngest I will ever be. My time, just as every other person's time, is now. Now is each person's gift, a pliable moment we can form and fashion according to our purpose and desires.

Most importantly, I feel spiritually connected to "the other side" because I know I am going to be passing the threshold soon. Well, maybe not soon, but certainly within the next twenty or thirty years. I feel part of me is already there, as I wonder and anticipate what is going to happen next. My new adventure will soon begin...

What is there not to love about being old?

www.ingramcontent.com/pod-product-compliance
Lightning Source LLC
Chambersburg PA
CBHW020914090426
42736CB00008B/625

* 9 7 8 0 9 8 1 5 5 0 9 6 1 *